Signs in My World

Signs at the Airport

By Mary Hill

Children's Press®
A Division of Scholastic Inc.
New York / Toronto / London / Auckland / Sydney
Mexico City / New Delhi / Hong Kong
Danbury, Connecticut

Thanks to the Philadelphia International Airport

Photo Credits: Cover and all photos by Maura B. McConnell
Contributing Editor: Jennifer Silate
Book Design: Erica Clendening and Michelle Innes

Library of Congress Cataloging-in-Publication Data

Hill, Mary, 1977–
  Signs at the airport / by Mary Hill.
  p. cm. — (Signs in my world)
  Includes bibliographical references.
  Contents: Going to the airport — Parking lot sign — Terminal D.
  ISBN 0-516-24272-5 (lib. bdg.) — ISBN 0-516-24364-0 (pbk.)
  1. Airports—Juvenile literature. 2. Signs and signboards—Juvenile
literature. [1. Airports. 2. Traffic signs and signals. 3. Signs and
signboards.] I. Title. II. Series.

TL725.3.S47H55 2003
625.7'94—dc21

                                                    2002007940

Contents

My name is Pat.

Dad and I are going to pick up Mom from the **airport**.

She is coming home from a trip today.

5

Dad drives us to the airport.

He **parks** the car in the **parking lot**.

There is a **sign** that says, "U 6."

The sign will help us remember where we parked our car.

Inside the airport, we find a sign that says, "**Arrivals**."

There are **screens** below the sign.

They show what time airplanes come into the airport.

Arrivals

PAGE 1 OF 6

ORIGIN	FLT#	SCHD	STATUS	GATE
ALBANY	2124	859A	CANCELED	B2
ALBANY	769	1244P	ON TIME	C22
	*3519	1220P	ON TIME	F7
ATLANTA	238	1233P	ON TIME	B7
ATLANTIC CITY	*5480	905A	ARRIVED	F6
BALTIMORE	1444	842A	ARRIVED	C27
BALTIMORE	*3170	1022A	1057A	F19
BALTIMORE	*3593	1215P	ON TIME	F23
BANGOR	*3224	1230P	ON TIME	
BEDFORD MA.	*4461	1200P	ON TIME	
BINGHAMTON	*3670	110P	ON TIME	
BIRMINGHAM	*5769	912A	ARRIVED	F25
BOSTON	107	910A	ARRIVED	B15
BOSTON	1607	1017A	1000A	C29
BOSTON	1121	1110A	ON TIME	C19

9:28A   PAGE 1 OF 6   JUNE 28, 2002

PAGE 2 OF 6

ORIGIN	FLT#	SCHD	STATUS	GATE
BOSTON	1291	1215P	ON TIME	C25
BUFFALO	918	1249P	ON TIME	B2
BURLINGTON	993	1259P	ON TIME	B19
CHARLESTON	*4015	1240P	ON TIME	F33
CHARLOTTE	1864	948A	ARRIVED	B16
CHARLOTTE	306	1055A	1038A	B5
CHICAGO O'HARE	832	903A	ARRIVED	B4
CHICAGO O'HARE	962	1250P	ON TIME	*C18
CINCINNATI	*4800	840A	1009A	F29
CINCINNATI	*5000	1225P	ON TIME	F5
CLEVELAND	*5853	1230P	ON TIME	F26
COLUMBIA	*4099	1235P	ON TIME	F8
COLUMBUS	976	1159A	ON TIME	B10
DALLAS FT WORTH	972	1240P	ON TIME	C24
DENVER	140	1240P	1225P	C29

9:28A   PAGE 2 OF 6   JUNE 28, 2002

Dad finds Mom's plane on the screen.

He says that she will be in **Terminal** D.

There is a sign that says,
"Terminal D."

Mom will be there.

← Terminal D

15

Here is Mom.

"Welcome home!"

16

Terminal
D

17

This sign above me says, **"Baggage Claim."**

The baggage claim is where we will pick up Mom's bags.

We have Mom's bags.

Now, we can go home.

21

New Words

airport (**air**-port) a place where airplanes take off and land

arrivals (uh-**rye**-vuhlz) things that have reached a place

baggage claim (**bag**-ij **klaym**) an area in an airport where travelers pick up their bags

parks (**parks**) when someone leaves a car or other vehicle in a space, in a garage, or at the curb of a street

parking lot (**park**-ing **lot**) a large space where cars can be parked

screens (**skreenz**) the front, flat parts of televisions or computers that you look at to see pictures or words

sign (**sine**) a public notice giving information

terminal (**tur**-muh-nuhl) a station at either end of a transportation line

To Find Out More

Books
Behind the Scenes at the Airport
by Marilyn Miller
Raintree/Steck Vaughn

The Airport
by Stuart A. Kallen
Checkerboard Library

Web Site
The Federal Aviation Administration: Kids Corner
http://www.faa.gov/education/resource/kidcornr.htm
Learn about flying, print out pictures to color, and play games
on this Web site.

Index

About the Author
Mary Hill writes and edits children's books.

Reading Consultants
Kris Flynn, Coordinator, Small School District Literacy, The San Diego County
  Office of Education

Shelly Forys, Certified Reading Recovery Specialist, W.J. Zahnow Elementary
  School, Waterloo, IL

Sue McAdams, Former President of the North Texas Reading Council of the
  IRA, and Early Literacy Consultant, Dallas, TX